Gigi Can't Remember

Written by Debra J. Frazier

Illustrated by Maryna Salagub

Grammy Gran is my Mom's grandma. She was a little girl a long, long time ago. When Grammy Gran was little there weren't any TV's, computers or cell phones.

My Grammy Gran didn't even have a refrigerator!
A lot of things were different when my Gigi, that's
what I call her, was my age.

When my Mom was a little girl, Gigi took care of her when
my Grammy worked.

Gigi would fix my Moms curly hair into perfect curly ponytails.
She taught my Mom how to speak Spanish and how to sew.

Gigi and Mom would stay up late at night talking and watching movies. My Mom loves my Gigi. Gigi even made my Mom special doll clothes for her dolls.

But that was a long, time ago...

I wish I had known my Gigi a long time ago. I love
Gigi and I know she loves me, but sometimes she
can't even remember my name.

My Mom helps my Grammy take care of Gigi.
Mom told me Gigi has a very hard time with
her memory.

I don't understand it...

Gigi tells me lots of stories about when she was a little girl. I love her stories! Sometimes she says the same thing over and over again.

My Mom says that's because Gigi has a sickness called Alzheimer's.

Sometimes Gigi gets pretty upset. Grammy says that Gigi is not upset with us. She gets upset because she can't remember things.

I get sad when Gigi is upset, but I get sad mostly because Gigi is changing.

We like to take Gigi shopping because she can't drive her car anymore. I like spending time with my Grammy and Gigi.

MALL
Grandmas Favourites

We watch old movies and Gigi talks about seeing them in the movie theater when she was my age.

We play old music and swing dance in the kitchen.
Gigi sings the songs she remembers.

I love it when Gigi remembers. But Gigi doesn't remember as much anymore.

My Mom fixes Gigi's hair and Grammy washes her clothes.

We make Gigi her favorite foods to help her eat better because she doesn't get hungry anymore. Mom says it is part of her sickness. We have to remind Gigi to drink water because she forgets. Grammy bought her a special water bottle with a flashing light on it to help her remember.

Sometimes I feel a little upset, maybe jealous, because
Mom and Grammy spend so much time caring for Gigi
and we don't have as much time together.

I try to help Gigi too. I help her remember how to change the channels on the TV with the remote.

And how to play games on her tablet.

We like to put puzzles together and Gigi puts the pieces in perfect little piles.

I try to help Gigi remember but she gets upset
if I remind her too much.

I like holding Gigi's hand. Her skin is so soft.
Sometimes she has purple dots on her hands.
Mom say it's from her medicine.

Grammy gives Gigi her medicine in the morning, at lunchtime and at bedtime.

Some of her pills help her heart and some help her memory. I wish they worked better.

And I wish there was a pill that would help Gigi not to be so cold. She's even cold when it's hot outside. She wears a sweater in the summertime.

I love my Gigi, but sometimes having a Grammy Gran that can't remember makes me sad.

I wish I knew my Gigi a long time ago, but it makes me happy to enjoy time with my Gigi today.

Gigi Can't Remember